1

Sonny and Manda lived in the same woods,
so they went to the same school. Every school
day, Sonny would walk to Manda's house and wait
for her.

Every day Sonny would call, "Let's go, slowpoke!"
Then Manda would come through the door, run
down the steps, and off to school they'd go.

One day Sonny was playing tag with the boys.

Winky yelled, "Let's race with two on each side —
everyone pick your best friend!"

Winky picked Tock, Zippy picked Jog, and Flip
picked Acey.

But no one picked Sonny. Sonny didn't have a
best friend.

That day while Sonny and Manda walked home, Sonny was quiet.

Then he said, "I wish I had a best friend."

"Why?" asked Manda.

Sonny said, "Because everyone at school has a best friend."

"I need a friend to have fun with, to play with
all the time," said Sonny.

Manda said, "We have fun and play together all
the time. We run and jump in the woods, we float
your boat in the lake, and we put on clown shows
together. We must be best friends!"

"I don't think so," said Sonny. "I'm a boy, so I need
a boy for a best friend. And you need a girl for your
best friend, Manda."

Manda said, "Mom, do I have a best friend?"

"You have a lot of friends, Manda," said her mom.
"There's Hedda, and Tottie, and Prin too.
But I think your best friend is Sonny. You two have
so much fun together!"

"That's what I think too," said Manda. "But Sonny said
he has to have a boy best friend."

Her mom said, "Maybe you are best friends,
and Sonny just doesn't know it yet. Let's wait and see."

Soon school was over, and Manda took a trip with
her family. They stayed away from home for a long time.

Every day Sonny went by Manda's house to see
if she was home yet. Then he would go play with Tock
or Flip or Manny. Sonny had fun, but not as much fun
as he had when he was with Manda.

Then one day Sonny heard that Manda had come home. He started to go to her house, but Manda had started to go to his house. So they met in the woods.

"Hi!" said Manda.

"Hi, Manda," Sonny said. "It's great to see you again!"

"Did you miss me?" asked Manda. "Or did you have too much fun playing with your best friend?"

"Well, I had fun, but not that much fun," said Sonny.

"Why not?" asked Manda.

And Sonny said, "Because my best friend was away on a trip with her family!"

Sonny and Manda looked at each other and smiled.

Then Sonny said, "Do you want to go down to the lake and play with my boat?"

And Manda said, "Or do you want to come over to my house and put on a clown show together?"

"I know," said Sonny. "First we'll do one, then we'll do the other!"

And that's what they did.